USING COMPUTER SCIENCE IN ONLINE RETAIL
» CAREERS «

CARLA MOONEY

Rosen
YA™

New York

Published in 2018 by The Rosen Publishing Group, Inc.
29 East 21st Street, New York, NY 10010

Library of Congress Cataloging-in-Publication Data

Names: Mooney, Carla, 1970– author.
Title: Using computer science in online retail careers / Carla Mooney.
Description: New York : Rosen Publishing, 2018. | Series: Coding your passion | Includes bibliographical references and index.
Identifiers: LCCN 2017001524 | ISBN 9781508175193 (library bound book)
Subjects: LCSH: Retail trade—Vocational guidance—Juvenile literature. | Electronic commerce—Juvenile literature. | Computer science—Vocational guidance—Juvenile literature.
Classification: LCC HF5429.29 .M66 2018 | DDC 658.8/72—dc23
LC record available at https://lccn.loc.gov/2017001524

Manufactured in China

CONTENTS

INTRODUCTION

The department store Neiman Marcus is well known for its high-end brick and mortar stores. Like many other retailers, Neiman Marcus also has a website where customers can buy items online. For many retailers, using technology means finding a way to increase online sales. For companies like Neiman Marcus, technology is being used to create an overall shopping experience, one that combines brick and mortar stores, online sales, and mobile devices. With technology, Neiman Marcus aims to create a new shopping experience for its customers. At the same time, the company hopes to gain more information about its customers.

To develop technology for its retail business, Neiman Marcus has set up an innovation lab called iLab. "A lot of [what we're doing] has been about try-ing to bring the things that online has to offer into the store," said Scott Emmons, enterprise architect of the iLab in a January 2016 *Computerworld* article. "I think it's safe to say our e-comm team has been on the leading edge, taking advantage of technologies as they come along and mature. What I do see happening is we are focused on taking advantage of delivering new experiences in the store, too."

Neiman Marcus has been testing Bluetooth bea-cons in some of its physical stores. A beacon is a

Traditional brick and mortar retailers like Neiman Marcus are developing apps that work with a shopper's smartphone to coordinate the online and in-person shopping experience.

wireless node that acts like a GPS locator and communicates with an app on a customer's phone. The beacon technology can guide the customer to in-store sales. Neiman Marcus is using beacons to integrate online and offline shopping even more. Using information gathered from its website, the company has data about a customer's browsing and shopping history. When the customer visits a physical store, the store's beacons recognize the customer via a smartphone app. The app can tell the customer where to find the item he or she had looked at online. The app can also alert the customer to sales or inform the cashier that the customer qualifies for a loyalty discount. "You place [beacons] throughout the store and then your mobile app can react to the customer's location," said Emmons in the *Computerworld* article. "We know you're at my door, walking through it, so I can appropriately greet and message you. We can know when you're two feet from something. You might be at checkout, and we could make an additional offer. We might say, 'Hey, you're near the restaurant and there's a chef there signing cookbooks today.'"

In 2015, Neiman Marcus tested beacon technology in three stores. In 2016, the retailer is building out the app technology and plans to run a more detailed test in a Dallas store.

The internet is changing the way people shop, research products, and make purchases. Online retail sales have steadily increased between 2011 and 2015, from $194.3 billion in 2011 to $341.7 billion in 2015. In addition, the rise of mobile technologies and smartphones creates even more opportunities for online retail. More than just having a website for sales, companies are increasingly finding ways to use technology to make the customer experience quicker, simpler, and more convenient. They are also using technology to combine online and offline sales, making the entire shopping experience more convenient for users.

People with an interest in retail and technology work for companies all over the world. There are many different career specialties that students can pursue. Retail companies employ software programmers, web developers, data scientists, marketing professionals, and more. With so many opportunities, online retail careers can fit many backgrounds and interests.

CHAPTER ONE

WHAT IS ONLINE RETAIL?

It's 6 a.m. on Tuesday morning. No stores are open, but that's not a problem for online shoppers. With a few clicks of the mouse, a shopper browses black boots from a few different companies. She compares prices and reads user reviews. With this information, she makes her choice. A few more clicks and she completes her purchase. The boots will be shipped to her home, arriving in a few days.

CHANGING HOW PEOPLE SHOP

The internet has changed the way people shop. Consumers can directly buy goods or services over the internet instead of purchasing them in a physical store. They can shop at any time, from any place. All they need is a device connected to the internet—a computer, laptop, tablet, or smartphone. Even people

While sitting on the couch in her living room, a woman opens her laptop, connects to the internet, and makes an online purchase without leaving the comfort of her home.

who do not regularly buy products online use the internet. They search and compare product prices, read information, check user reviews, and check availability before heading out to the store. "Customers now want to be able to buy anything, at competitive prices and delivered quickly," says Conrad Chua, head of MBA careers at the University of Cambridge in England, in a 2014 article on BusinessBecause.com.

More and more customers are going online to make purchases. According to a 2016 report from Forrester Research, a technology and market research company, online retail sales in the United States are expected to reach $373 billion in 2016. The report predicts that US online retail will grow to more than $500 billion by 2020. By 2020, 270 million consumers are expected to be shopping online. Many of them will be using mobile devices such as tablets and smartphones. "Screen sizes for mobile phones have gradually increased in size and wireless networks are better than before, which has made web browsing easier than ever," says Forrester principal analyst Sucharita Mulpuru in an article on Internet Retailer in January 2016. "Additionally, consumers are more accustomed to using their phones everywhere and shopping is a byproduct of that ubiquity."

THE RISE OF ONLINE RETAIL

Only twenty to thirty years ago, most people did not even know that you could shop on the internet. The invention of the World Wide Web in 1991 allowed the average person to easily access and use the internet. In 1995, Amazon launched a website as an online book seller. At first, people were skeptical about buying books online when a person could get the same item at the local bookstore. Soon people realized that they could use the internet to easily compare and find the best price on an item. And the internet opened the door for a much broader selection of items. If a person lived in a small town with a single bookstore, he or she could turn to the internet to order a book that was not in stock.

During the busy holiday shopping season, workers at an Amazon fulfillment center in Peterborough, England, are busy processing and packaging the purchases made by online shoppers.

At first, online retail grew with products that people did not have to touch, feel, or smell to buy. Books, computers, and other electronics were popular internet sellers. As more people became comfortable shopping online, retailers expanded their offerings. Stores launched websites so that they could sell products in stores and online.

Today, almost anything that a person can buy can be bought online. "As the Internet has evolved, it's become a channel where you can buy anything," says Ellen Davis, a vice president with the National Retail

Federation, in a 2010 Time.com article. "You can buy fragrances — something you would have normally thought you would need to go to a store and actually experience before you decided to buy." Since its beginning, online retail has grown into an industry with billions of dollars in sales.

HOW ONLINE RETAIL WORKS

For a customer, online shopping is fairly simple. Once shoppers decide what they want to buy, they click to purchase. Then they enter some information such as credit card numbers and delivery address into a web form. A few days later, the purchase arrives at their door.

Behind the scenes, a lot of technology operates to get the right package to the customer on time. Different software and technologies allow retailers to build a digital storefront that sells products or services. This platform can be integrated with other company software such as inventory management, customer relationship management, or shipping software. Web developers and programmers create the websites that customers see. Programmers write applications for payment systems that are integrated into the website. Other technology experts design the systems used by warehouse workers and delivery companies to make sure the right product is delivered to the right customer, on time.

TECHNOLOGY FOR A BETTER SHOPPING EXPERIENCE

The latest technologies are making online shopping even better for customers and companies. Mobile apps allow customers to shop on their smartphones. Data analytics help companies gather information about a customer's shopping habits so that they can offer suggestions of items the customer is likely to want.

Other technologies focus on the shopping experience. Many companies are using image-interactive technology to display products on their websites. This technology allows shoppers to interact with the product virtually. They can zoom and rotate it. Some clothing websites even show a model walking in the apparel.

WORKING IN ONLINE RETAIL

For people who want to combine working in retail with an interest in technology, online retail may be a great career option. The growth in online retail has opened the door for people who are interested in working with retail technology and want to improve and create more systems and technology. Companies need qualified information technology professionals, software developers, and internet-savvy employees who can work in the online marketplace. Performing a variety of roles, these people create innovative and convenient ways

The online retail industry relies on people with an interest in computer science who have strong technical skills and are Internet-savvy to create innovative and creative shopping experiences.

for people to shop online and help companies beat their competitors.

Having strong computer science skills is essential for most online retail careers. Many people working in online retail have a computer science degree. A few have degrees in marketing, mathematics, or statistics. No matter their degree, people working in online retail need to have a knowledge of retail systems, databases, systems, and web technology. Knowledge of programming languages such as Java, JavaScript, Python, R, CSS, and HTML are valuable.

JavaScript is primarily used to build websites and create a better user experience. It is also an essential skill for building Android apps. Python is another common programming language used in online retail platforms. Programmers use Python to build analytic tools and develop models. Knowing R language is another helpful skill. This software is used for calculations and data analysis. CSS is a programming language used to design the format and layout of a website.

In addition to technical skills, retail employers are looking for people who have other skills in business and project management. For many online retail careers, the ability to work well together and communicate is critical. Many positions require a person to think innovatively to solve problems and meet customer needs.

BENEFITS AND DRAWBACKS

Online retail offers many benefits to consumers. Its convenience cannot be beat, with shoppers able to browse items and make purchases from any place, at any time, as long as they are connected to the internet. Also, online shoppers have access to products from around the world. They are no longer restricted to the products that their local stores carry. With the internet, consumers can purchase tea from China or wool sweaters from Ireland. They can also compare products from different companies and stores, finding the best price or reading reviews from people who already purchased the items.

(continued on the next page)

(continued from the previous page)

At the same time, there are some drawbacks to shopping online. Customers enter personal information such as addresses, birthdates, and credit card or bank account numbers into website forms. In some cases, hackers have been able to breach the company's systems to steal this information. In 2016, technology manufacturer Acer reported that hackers had gotten into its online store's system and stolen a year's worth of credit card data, names, and addresses of its customers. The theft of personal information puts the customer at risk of identity theft.

PURSUING A CAREER IN ONLINE RETAIL

People who are interested in an online retail career should take classes to give them solid technical computer and programming skills. Some people choose to get a computer-related degree from a four-year college or university. Others who have degrees in another field attend special coding boot camps or technology-focused graduate programs. For some specialties, earning a certificate is a good way to show that a person has the skills needed for the career.

In addition to taking classes, people interested in an online retail career can take other steps to learn more about the industry. Joining a retail, business, or

Students work together in a computer lab to practice technical and computer programming skills that they will be able to use in an online retail career.

marketing society can help a person learn more about marketing and the retail industry and make contacts in these industries. Some companies offer internships to students. Internships give students the experience of working for a particular company or industry. Reading newspapers and other business and technology publications can help students keep up to date on the latest developments in retail and technology.

CHAPTER TWO

WEB DEVELOPMENT AND DESIGN

E ach year, more people go online to purchase goods and services. According to Forrester Research, approximately 270 million people will be shopping online by 2020. In order to attract potential customers, a company needs to have a state-of-the art website. Through its website, it can provide customers with efficient and secure ways to browse products and make purchases.

A WELL-DESIGNED WEBSITE

Customers visit a company's website to learn more about products, find store locations, and buy products. They research information about products and read customer reviews. Having a website is an important way to get a company's products in front of customers. However, just having a site is not enough. Retailers need to make sure their sites are well-designed and user friendly. Some of the best retail websites incorporate features such as

Online shoppers often use internet search engines like Google to find company websites and search for information and customer reviews about products they are interested in purchasing.

graphics, videos, and other applications. Also, retailers need to make sure that their site is being picked up by the online search engines and review sites.

Without a website, retailers miss out on sales. Customers cannot find them and decide if they want to purchase their products or services. Instead, the customers simply move on to the next company that has a website. In some cases, having a bad website may be worse than having no website at all. A bad website can make a company look unprofessional and sloppy. Customers are turned off and take their business elsewhere.

WEB DEVELOPMENT AND DESIGN

Web developers create specialized eye-catching websites for the retail industry. Retail web developers often use color, images, layout, photos, and fonts to create a stylish website. Because every company is different, web developers work with each company to create an individual design that appeals to its customers. Web developers then take their design and create a website. After the site is built, they adjust or add updates to the site regularly.

Toys Paradise is a toy retailer in Australia. At first, the company sold its merchandise only from a physical store. The owners quickly realized that most customers searched for product information online to help their buying decisions. These customers also started to buy more toys online because it was more convenient than going to the physical store. Toys Paradise decided to follow customers online and launch a website. They hired a website development firm that specialized in retail clients. For the website, the developers used state-of-the-art technology that allowed the company to integrate the site with their existing inventory and accounting systems. In five months, the site went live. The company immediately saw an increase in sales in just the first month. By the end of the year, they reached over $1 million in sales. Using data from the website, the toy retailer also built a customer database of over fifteen thousand customers.

WORKING AS A WEB DEVELOPER IN ONLINE RETAIL

Web developers design and create websites. They are responsible for the site's appearance and its technical features. These include the site's performance or speed and its capacity, which is the amount of user traffic it can handle. Some web developers also create content for sites.

In a typical day, a web developer might meet with clients or coworkers to talk about the function and design of a website. They write code for websites, often using programming languages such as HTML, CSS, and JavaScript. They create and test applications for the site. They work with other team members and designers to determine a site's information, function, and layout. They incorporate graphics, audio, and video into the site. Once the site is up and running, web developers monitor traffic, make adjustments or additions as necessary, and troubleshoot any problems.

Web developers customize websites for a customer or company's needs. Different types of websites need different applications to work correctly. For example, a retail site should have an integrated ordering application. Working with the rest of the product development team, the web developer determines which applications and design work best for the site.

While some web developers handle every part of a website's construction from design to maintenance, others specialize in certain areas. Back-end web

Two web designers brainstorm ideas while creating a new website mockup. When finished, they will present the proposed website design to the client for approval.

developers focus on how a site operates. They oversee the website's technical construction. They create the site's basic framework and make sure that it works as designed. Back-end developers also determine the process for adding new pages and information to the website. In contrast, front-end web developers focus more on how a site looks and how users interact with it. They create layouts and integrate graphics, applications, and other content. Front-end developers often write web programs in computer languages such as HTML or JavaScript. Once a website is up and running, webmasters maintain and update them.

HOW TO BECOME A WEB DEVELOPER

Most web developers have at least an associate's degree in web design or a related field. For more technical jobs, some employers want employees to have at least a bachelor's degree in computer science, programming, or a related field. Taking courses in graphic design can also be helpful, especially if the web developer will be involved in creating a website's visual appearance.

Web developers should have strong technical and web programming skills. They must be proficient in HTML, the markup language for making web pages. Developers should also have strong technical skills in other programming languages, such as JavaScript and CSS, and be able to work with multimedia publishing tools such as Flash. Because the computer science environment is always changing, web developers must continue to develop new computer skills and stay current on new tools and programming languages. Mike Feineman, the lead developer at Room 214, a social media agency, recommends that students showcase their abilities in personal projects. "It doesn't need to be your grand opus. Take a weekend and build something you've been thinking about. A working demo proves you can get things done, and that will take you a long way," he says in a 2013 interview on Aftercollege.com.

In addition to strong technical skills, web developers should also have several other qualities and skills to be successful. Because web developers often spend a lot of time at a computer, writing detailed code for hours, the ability to concentrate and focus on small details is extremely important. A tiny error in the HTML code could cause an entire webpage to stop working. Successful web developers are often very creative people, which can help them design a website's appearance and make sure it is innovative and fresh. Web developers should also have excellent communication and interpersonal skills to communicate effectively with coworkers, management, and clients.

RESPONSIVE DESIGN

One of the hottest trends in retail website design is responsive design. No longer are customers simply looking at websites on a computer screen. Today, they use smartphones, tablets, laptops, and other mobile devices to go online and browse websites. For many companies, this means designing and developing websites that work for each of these devices and screen sizes. As the number of devices is only expected to increase in the future, it will soon be impossible to keep up designing new websites for each one. The idea of responsive web design may solve that problem. Responsive web design is the idea that design and development should respond to a user's behavior and environment. Designing a website with a mix of flexible grids, layouts, images, and more allows it to be viewed from different screen sizes, platforms, and orientations. As users switch from their smartphone to an iPad, the website automatically switches to account for the change in resolution, screen size, and other qualities. This eliminates the need to design a new website for each device introduced to the market.

JOB OUTLOOK

The job outlook for web developers is very good. According to the Bureau of Labor Statistics' *Occupational Outlook Handbook*, employment of web developers is projected to grow 27 percent from 2014 to 2024. This rate of growth is much faster than the average of all occupations. In online retail, this growth is driven by the rapid increase in online platforms and services for consumers. As retail stores expand their online offerings, demand for web developers will continue to increase. In addition, the growing use of mobile devices will also increase the number of opportunities as developers will be needed to create sites that work on mobile devices and multiple screen

In a job interview, a web developer candidate highlights her computer programming and technical skills and answers questions about her previous experience in web development.

sizes. Candidates who have strong technical skills and knowledge of multiple programming languages and digital multimedia tools will have the best opportunities for working as a web developer in the online retail industry.

CHAPTER THREE

MOBILE APPS

With a smartphone and an internet connection, consumers can research products, search for coupons, and make a purchase anywhere, at any time. "Mobile devices are driving demand," said Andrew Lipsman, a comScore vice president who has studied mobile shopping, in a *Wall Street Journal* article in April 2016. "They can create an impulsive buying moment at any point in the day because they are with you all the time, right in your pocket."

REACHING CUSTOMERS THROUGH APPS

Because consumers increasingly are going online with smartphones, retailers are developing technology to reach them through their phones. One of the easiest ways to reach consumers over their phones is through

Using her smartphone, a young woman connects to the Internet and uses mobile apps to browse company websites and make purchases from the palm of her hand.

a mobile app. A mobile app is a software application that is developed specifically to be used on small, mobile devices such as smartphones and tablets, instead of being run on desktop or laptop computers. Users can use apps to play games, get directions, access news, read books, and more. They are easy to download and usually free.

For online retail, some mobile apps allow customers to browse products and make a purchase. Other apps help shoppers save money or have a better experience. For example, apps like Checkout 51 let shoppers collect online coupons that can be redeemed from their mobile phone. Apps can alert shoppers to special offers via push notifications or use beacon technology to personalize a shopping experience. Some apps even allow customers to make payments from their smartphones.

Hana Pugh, a twenty-nine-year-old event planner, says that she buys most of her household items using apps on her iPhone. Pugh frequently uses Amazon's app to buy essentials such as diapers for her family. "It's quicker to pull out my phone and click 'buy' than to log on to my computer," said Pugh in an article that appeared in the *Wall Street Journal* in April 2016.

The popularity of mobile apps is steadily increasing. Consumers are downloading more retail apps to their phones and mobile devices than ever before. According to a comScore custom survey, 21 percent of respondents said that they had between six and ten retail apps on their phone as of April 2016, while another 16 percent had eleven or more apps on their phone. Nineteen-year-old Olivia Bryant from California says that she spends up to two hours a day shopping on her iPhone using apps such as marketplace Etsy Inc. and fashion retailer Poshmark Inc. "It's much simpler to shop on my phone," she said in a *Wall Street Journal* article in April 2016. "There aren't a lot of distractions."

In 2016, Amazon used its Prime Now app and beacon technology to deliver products to NFL fans tailgating in certain parking lots at the San Francisco 49ers Levi's Stadium in Santa Clara, California. Fans can open the app and enter the stadium's zip code to see tens of thousands of products available for quick delivery. They click to make a purchase and then enter the stadium's address, parking lot number, and nearest parking flag number in the delivery notes. Amazon promises the product will arrive within one hour for a small fee. For now, the service is limited to fans in certain parking lots.

WORKING AS A MOBILE APP DEVELOPER

Mobile app developers design and create the applications that allow people to perform specific tasks on a mobile device. Typically, mobile app developers begin by talking with customers or retail management to see what they need and how they plan to use the app. Through these discussions and other research, mobile app developers determine the core functions required in the app. They also determine other user requirements such as security and performance. With this information, developers design the app. For many projects, the developers write the code themselves. If the resulting application does not work as intended, mobile app developers tweak the design to fix any problems. After the application is released, developers may continue to improve it with upgrades.

As an app developer for a mobile app development company, Justin James has worked on many mobile apps for a variety of companies. In a March 2011 article in the *Guardian*, James said that creating an app is often easier said than done. "It can be straightforward

Two mobile app developers compare the look and feel of a company's smartphone app to its website on a laptop and ensure the app works smoothly for users.

or it can be difficult. With the Decanter wine app, we had a huge database of wines and regions that the user had to be able to access. We had to find a way of displaying that information quickly and we decided to force the app to access the internet to do it. Even then, that's a large chunk of data for a mobile phone to process so we had to find ways to slow the user down and stop them getting angry if it took too long to find what they wanted," he said.

CREATING A VIRTUAL CLOSET

An app called ClosetSpace from fashion analytics company Stylitics puts a digital closet on a person's phone. The app serves as a centralized fashion hub and helps users manage their style and find new things to wear. Users can take photos and tag items from their own closets or add them from a retailer's catalog. These items can be used in the app's personalized style recommendations. The app gives users access to a network of more than 140 fashion bloggers to give fashion ideas. There is even an on-demand pro stylist available for a monthly fee. The stylist will suggest ten outfits to users and show them where to buy them. Also, ClosetSpace can connect users with offers and deals from retailers based on their existing closet items. In the future, the company hopes to add more features to the ClosetSpace hub, such as giving users the ability to shop and sell items in a secondhand fashion store. The app also feeds data to Stylitics' paying company customers. They receive real-time data about changing fashion trends.

HOW TO BECOME A MOBILE APP DEVELOPER

Most software and mobile app developers have at least a bachelor's degree in computer science, software engineering, or a related field from a four-year college or university. Although not all developers write code, students should take classes to develop software computer programming skills. They should have strong skills in Java and HTML. They should also understand modern object-oriented programming, user interfaces, and design patterns. Taking courses in marketing, business, and retail are also recommended.

Experience working with mobile app coding can also help. Mobile app developers should be familiar with the major mobile platforms, particularly Android and Apple. Online development programs such as iOS Dev Center or the Android Developers Training site can help students learn coding. Other free online courses and websites also offer coding training.

A computer science teacher answers a question for a student as he learns HTML, Java, and other computer programming skills.

Mobile app developers need to have a firm grasp of the difference between designing an app for a smartphone and a program for a desktop computer. Not only do smartphones have smaller screen sizes, consumers use them differently than computers. "The way people interact with a laptop or a desktop is different than the way they interact with a smart device," says Hap Aziz, director of the Rasmussen College School of Technology and Design in an article in *Computerworld* in June 2011. "People using a smart device don't think of themselves as 'computer users,' therefore you can't use the same conventions you'd use in developing desktop software. Drop-down menus and elaborate help screens just don't work on a smart device —it's more like working an ATM machine at the bank."

Throughout their career, mobile app developers must continue to develop their computer skills and stay current on new tools and programming languages. There are numerous continuing education and certificate courses in subjects such as HTML5 and iOS and Android programming. Many professionals recommend that people who want to work as mobile app developers immerse themselves in mobile technology. Doing so can help them learn firsthand the opportunities and limits of mobile apps.

Getting firsthand experience is very beneficial for people interested in mobile app development. Some people get experience by designing their own app, which they can show to prospective employers. Others work as interns at large tech companies, where they learn the basics of app development and what it is like to work at a company. During an internship, students can make contacts that will help them identify future job opportunities.

In addition to strong computer skills, developers in the online retail industry should also have a knowledge of retail and marketing so that they can understand their company and customers' needs. Developers should also be creative, have good analytical skills, and be detail oriented. A good developer can analyze customer needs and develop a creative solution to meet those needs. Developers should also have excellent communication and interpersonal skills. Many developers work closely with others on a team. They must be able to communicate effectively with team members.

JOB OUTLOOK

The job outlook for software developers, including mobile app developers, is strong. According to the Bureau of Labor Statistics' *Occupational Outlook Handbook*, employment of software and mobile app developers is projected to grow 17 percent from 2014 to 2024. This rate of growth is much faster than the average for all occupations. One of the drivers of this growth is the need for new applications on mobile devices. Candidates who have strong skills in the most up-to-date programming tools and languages will have the best prospects for landing a good mobile app development job in the online retail industry.

CHAPTER FOUR

DATA ANALYTICS

With every click on a website, consumers leave a trail of information about their preferences and buying habits. Retailers use this online record to build a profile of their customers. They track how users found the website, how long they stayed, what pages they looked at, and what they purchased. Online forms gather personal details such as age, gender, and location. Retailers who can put all of this data into a meaningful format and analyze it can get a step ahead of their competitors. They can use data to improve the shopping experience and satisfy customers.

HOW ONLINE RETAILERS USE DATA

Online shoppers want a personalized experience when they go online. They expect up-to-date and on-demand information and superior customer service. Online retailers use data collected online to meet these needs.

A data scientist organizes large amounts of company, customer, and product data into a massive computer database which can be used to access specific information for analysis.

Data allows online retailers to price products and services effectively. With dynamic pricing, companies can gather data about competitor pricing and adjust their own prices as needed. They gather pricing information from multiple sources such as competitor websites, product sales, and regional stores. Amazon changes the prices on some items as many as ten times per day.

Data also gives retailers the ability to personalize every interaction with a customer. If a retailer knows that a customer has purchased several murder mystery novels, it can recommend newly released mystery books to them. At Amazon, the company uses big data to recommend products. Customers see recommendations for additional products based on what they are currently browsing online. This feature increased sales by nearly 30 percent when it was first added to the company's website.

Companies can also use data to predict industry trends. Clothing retailers can analyze customer data to identify the most popular fabrics and styles. They use this information to order new inventory. Some online retailers use social media and other sources to track what customers are buying. Record company EMI uses data from third-party sites and apps to analyze customer listening and buying patterns. With this information, it predicts product demand and targets advertising to the audiences most likely to buy its music.

Sometimes, online shoppers click to add an item to their shopping cart but then leave the site without finalizing their purchase. This phenomenon is known as shopping cart abandonment. Some online retailers are using data to reduce shopping cart abandonment. Through tracking how customers accessed their website, Ebay discovered that the average shopper used as many as three to five devices during the buying process. This information helped the company design applications that allow customers to transition from one device to another without losing their shopping cart.

WORKING AS A DATA SCIENTIST

In online retail, every retailer needs to understand its customers through data. Online retail companies need data scientists to make sense of all the data they receive and put it into a useful and understandable format. They use their skills in math, statistics, and computer science to gather and organize enormous amounts of data. Then they use analytical skills and industry knowledge to find solutions for the business. A data scientist writes algorithms to analyze large amounts of data. They build predictive models and software to help a company make decisions about inventory, advertising, promotions, and more.

Each day, data scientists may perform a variety of tasks. They conduct research on industry questions. They extract huge volumes of data from a variety of sources. They operate sophisticated analytics programs and statistical methods to prepare data for predictive modeling. They use software programs to cleanse data and eliminate irrelevant information. They examine the data from different perspectives to identify trends, opportunities, and weaknesses. They create algorithms to solve problems and build tools to automate work. They also prepare reports that communicate their findings and results for management.

Some jobs will focus more on data analytics—collecting and processing statistical analyses of data, and using the information to answer questions and solve problems. Other jobs require data scientists to build massive databases for big data information. They develop, build, test, and maintain these databases and data processing systems. Once these systems are built, data scientists can use them to access specific data for analysis.

As data scientists gain more experience, their

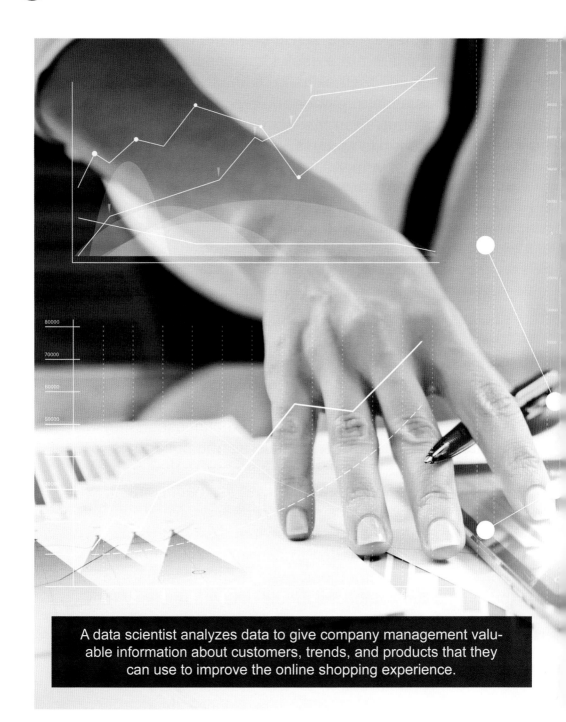

A data scientist analyzes data to give company management valuable information about customers, trends, and products that they can use to improve the online shopping experience.

responsibilities often change. A person new to the job might spend most of the day cleaning data and preparing it for analysis. A more senior data scientist may spend more time designing big data projects or creating new company products.

HOW TO BECOME A DATA SCIENTIST

Most data scientists have a master's degree or PhD, in addition to a bachelor's degree. They often major in areas such as mathematics, statistics, or computer science. Taking courses in math and statistics prepares students to work in data scientist jobs. These courses can help students develop the technical skills they will need in linear algebra, calculus, probability, statistical hypothesis testing, and summary statistics. In addition, students should take courses to develop machine learning tools and techniques.

Computer science skills are critical for data scientists. Potential employees need to be able to work with data through data mining, cleaning and munging, and data visualization. They should also be proficient in programming languages such as Python, C/C++, Java, and Perl. They should be skilled in working with SQL databases and database querying languages. In addition, data scientists should develop skills to work with cloud tools such as Amazon S3. Because the computer science environment is always changing, data scientists must continue to develop new computer skills and stay current on new tools and programming languages.

In addition to strong technical skills, several additional skills are important for people working as data scientists. Data scientists in the online retail industry should have a knowledge of retail and marketing so that they can understand their company's and customers' needs. Problem-solving skills are also important because data scientists have to create new ways of looking at and analyzing data. Data scientists should have excellent communication and interpersonal skills. Many data scientists work closely with others in a team. The work is often spread among team members, and the ability to work well with others and communicate is essential. In addition, data scientists must be able to communicate effectively with management and others who may not have a technical background.

DATA ANALYTICS AT STITCH FIX

A personal stylist at Stitch Fix, an online personal styling service, reviews a customer profile and style recommendations based on the company's hundreds of algorithms.

Founded in 2011, Stitch Fix is an online personal styling service. Clients sign up for the service online. They answer questions about their style and fit preferences. Then a team of fashion stylists and data scientists work together to select five items to send the client. The client tries on the clothing and accessories at home. Clients keeps what they want and send back the rest.

To serve its clients, Stitch Fix relies on hundreds of algorithms. Styling algorithms match clients with

(continued on the next page)

(continued from the previous page)

products. Algorithms match stylists with clients. Another algorithm calculates how satisfied a client is with the service, while another algorithm determines how much and what type of inventory Stitch Fix should buy. Stitch Fix even has an algorithm that checks a client's Pinterest page to see what styles the client likes. The company's algorithms constantly incorporate new data from client purchases and feedback. The company's algorithms use machine learning and get more accurate as they handle more data. The algorithms make recommendations for a client to one of Stitch Fix's human stylists. The stylist then makes the final decision on what to send the client.

JOB OUTLOOK

The job outlook for data scientists is very good. According to the Bureau of Labor Statistics' *Occupational Outlook Handbook*, employment of computer and information research scientists is projected to grow 11 percent from 2014 to 2024. This rate of growth is faster than the average for all occupations. In retail, this growth is driven by the rapid increase in data collection by companies and a resulting increased need for data-mining services. Computer data scientists will be needed to write algorithms to help online retail businesses understand large amounts of data. With this information, companies can understand their customers better.

Many companies report difficulty finding these highly skilled workers. Therefore, the job prospects for data scientists are good. Candidates who have strong technical and analytical skills in the most up-to-date programming tools and languages will have the best prospects for landing a good data scientist job in the online retail industry.

CHAPTER FIVE

DIGITAL MARKETING

M arketing connects companies with potential customers at the right place, at the right time. Today, the internet has become a critical tool for pre-shopping research and making purchases. As a result, many retail companies are directing more of their marketing efforts to the internet.

Digital marketing includes all online marketing efforts. Companies use online tools such as search engines, social media, email, and websites to connect with customers. They design eye-catching, memorable content to get their products and services noticed by potential customers. They design digital advertising campaigns, email campaigns, and pay-per-click cam-paigns. They create easy-to-read online brochures. They add engaging content and interactive tools to websites and blogs. They place ads in games and mobile apps. They are active on social media channels like Facebook, LinkedIn, Twitter, and Instagram. They

Popular social media services such as Instagram and Facebook have become a new channel for online retail marketers to reach potential customers through their smartphones.

design pay-per-click campaigns that appear on search engine sites. Each of these digital marketing activities is designed to get people to visit a company's website, buy a product or service, and come back later.

SEARCH ENGINE OPTIMIZATION

When a person searches for "toy stores" on a search engine like Google, the engine returns a list of websites. Potential customers are more likely to click on a website link near the top of the list. Therefore, the higher a company can be listed in the search engine's results, the more potential customers will find its website.

A digital marketing technique called search engine optimization (SEO) gets a company's website to appear higher on search engine lists. Search engines like Google use a complex mathematical algorithm to give a score to each website. They use the scores to rank sites and figure out which ones best match a person's search. SEO is a strategy to tailor a website so that it scores higher in the search engine's algorithm. SEO may involve editing a website's content and HTML coding to increase the use of keywords and its search engine score. It may also involve increasing the number of inbound links or links from other pages to the website.

SOCIAL MEDIA MARKETING

According to a 2016 survey by Statista, 78 percent of Americans had a social media profile, a 5 percent increase since 2015. As social media platforms such as Twitter, Facebook, LinkedIn, and YouTube become more popular, many retail businesses have incorporated these sites into their digital marketing strategy.

The goal of social media marketing is to develop an online presence and attract a high number of internet followers. One way companies do that is by creating content that users will share with their social networks. When people share a company's content, it increases brand awareness, drives traffic to its websites, and attracts potential new customers. In fact, more than 90 percent of marketers say that social media marketing is an important part of their digital marketing strategy. American fashion brand Kate Spade is one example of a company that has invested in social media marketing. The company has built a large and loyal customer following on Facebook, Twitter, Pinterest, Instagram, Tumblr, and YouTube. On each channel, the company gives customers fresh and fun content and images. It chooses this content from research about what the customers like.

Like SEO, social media optimization (SMO) attempts to draw new visitors to a website. SMO adds social media links to content or promotes social media activity by posting updated statuses, tweeting, or creating blog posts. Social media sites are also revamping their platforms to make it easier for companies to market to customers. Facebook offers paid advertising services that target a specific audience from its billions of daily users. Companies use Twitter to send out news about the events and product releases. On LinkedIn, companies can promote a company profile and display ads.

On social media, companies also directly interact with customers. Customers can leave feedback about likes and dislikes. They can ask questions or post complaints. Companies can respond quickly and directly to customer comments.

WORKING AS A DIGITAL MARKETING MANAGER

Online retailers need marketers who can devise creative and innovative ways to get people to visit their websites, make a purchase, and come back again in the future. Digital marketing managers drive the design and implementation of a company's digital marketing strategy. They work with different people and departments within a company, such as sales and finance. They may also work with freelance web developers, graphic designers, and other professionals.

A marketing team works together to review a company's digital marketing strategy, which includes social media advertising, blog posts, email blasts, and search engine optimization.

Digital marketing managers design a company's marketing efforts across a variety of online channels, including websites, social media, email campaigns, mobile technology, and more. They meet with coworkers and customers to make sure that digital campaigns meet user and business needs. They ensure that the company's brand message is being appropriately used across all digital channels. They develop and send email campaigns. They evaluate the look and content of websites and plan how they will be used in campaigns and advertisements. They work with the web administrators and developers to make changes and enhancements to company websites. They need to stay up to date with new and emerging

CABLETV.COM ON SOCIAL MEDIA

CableTV.com is an online company that works with television and internet brands to show consumers the available cable providers in their areas. It helps consumers compare providers in their areas and make informed decisions about cable service. In addition, the company provides content to help consumers better understand the cable and internet industries. Cable TV.com uses social media to engage users. Its social media marketing campaign uses hashtags to promote television shows. The company also uses Google + to draw attention to followers and drive them to the CableTV.com blog.

(continued on the next page)

(continued from the previous page)

The company posts teaser headlines on its Facebook page that include interviews with TV series actors. Viewers post comments on the company's Facebook page, which gives them a good source of information about customer likes, preferences, and concerns.

digital technologies and understand current trends in digital media. They monitor, analyze, and adjust digital marketing campaigns to achieve the best outcomes. They also monitor digital channels to understand customer needs and concerns and to identify new opportunities for the company.

HOW TO BECOME A DIGITAL MARKETING MANAGER

Most digital marketing manager positions require a bachelor's degree from a four-year college or university. Some employers require a master's degree. Most people interested in this career path major in marketing, communications, digital marketing, or a related field. Regardless of major, courses in marketing, consumer behavior, market research, sales, and graphic design are helpful. Classes in finance, mathematics, and statistics are also good to take.

People in this career should also have strong computer and web skills. They should have experience using content management systems and working with digital media channels such as websites, apps, social media, blogs, and more. They should understand digital technology platforms, content strategies, search engine optimization strategies, and user experience (UX) best practices. They should also be familiar with Google analytics and other web measurement platforms. Some people choose to complete an internship while in school in order to gain firsthand experience and develop their technical skills. Some people choose to obtain certifications in different technical and coding skills.

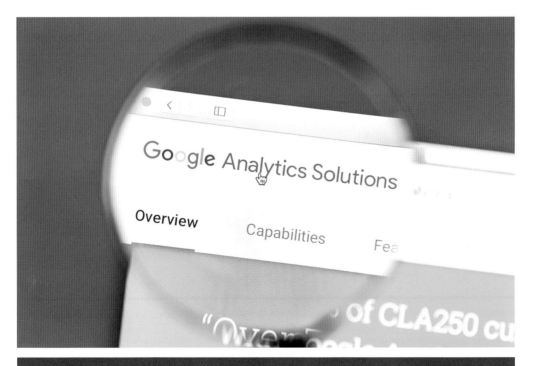

Offered by Google, Google Analytics is a web analytics service that helps a company measure website, app, digital, and offline data to better understand customers and markets.

In addition to strong technical skills, digital marketers should have a knowledge of the retail industry so that they can understand their company's and customers' needs. They should be able to identify customer needs and translate them into the appropriate digital marketing strategies. Problem-solving skills are also important because digital marketers have to create new ways of looking at and analyzing information. Digital marketers should have excellent communication and interpersonal skills. Many marketers work closely with others in a team. The work is often spread among team members and the ability to work well with others and communicate is essential. They must also be able to communicate effectively with the public and persuade people to visit the company's website and purchase products or services. In addition, digital marketers must be able to balance multiple projects and assignments at a time. They need to be able to meet the goals, budgets, and timelines of each project.

JOB OUTLOOK

The job outlook for digital marketing managers is very good. According to the Bureau of Labor Statistics' *Occupational Outlook Handbook*, employment of marketing managers is projected to grow 9 percent from 2014 to 2024. This rate of growth is faster than the average for all occupations. The continuing rise of the internet will drive the growth for digital marketing managers. They will be needed to target customers across many platforms, such as websites, social media, and mobile channels. As companies seek to market products to specific customers online, digital marketing managers will be in demand.

Marketing manager jobs are highly desired. As a result, strong competition is expected for these jobs. Candidates who have strong technical, analytical, and marketing skills and have experience with the retail and digital world will have the best opportunities.

CHAPTER SIX

USER/CUSTOMER EXPERIENCE

Most consumers shop online because they want to save time and avoid the hassle of a physical store. Therefore, it is critical that websites make the shopping process as quick and easy to understand as possible. Browsing products, comparing items, and checking out should be streamlined and simple. The site should give customers the information they need without overloading them with too many details or flashy graphics. While the look of a site may be designed to influence customer behavior, the user experience interacting with the site may be the biggest factor in whether or not the user makes a purchase or leaves empty-handed.

IMPROVING USER EXPERIENCE

There are several strategies that online retail companies use to improve user experience while online. User experience (UX) is defined as how a person feels when he or she interacts with a system, website, mobile app, or desktop software. In online retail, making sure that a company's website loads quickly is critical. Every second matters in e-commerce. Websites should load on a customer's computer or mobile device in a few seconds or less. If it loads too slowly, customers will leave. Therefore, online retailers need to optimize their websites to perform well on any device the customer uses to access it—a desktop, laptop, tablet, or phone. "Today's online customers want the information they need when they need it, at the click of a mouse or a swipe of a tablet or smartphone," says Ari Weil,

Online shoppers become frustrated when websites do not work smoothly and intuitively. Improving the user experience can create loyal customers who make future purchases from a website.

vice president of Yottaa, a cloud-based automation platform, in a 2015 interview with *CIO* magazine. "And retailers have only milliseconds to grab their attention and complete the transaction. Amazon, for example, has shown that every 100 milliseconds of latency cost them 1 percent in sales, while Walmart reports conversion rates rise 2 percent for every second of reduced load time." Good site navigation also impacts UX. Customers should be able to navigate easily and find what they need on a company's website. Customers should never be lost or confused on a retail website. If they must click too many times, they will lose interest. Thin fonts or low contrast on the site might make it hard to read. Good site search technology can be an easy way to help users find what they need.

Simple checkout is another part of creating a good UX. When purchasing online, users add items to their shopping cart. Making the shopping cart process simple, streamlined, and easy is essential to completing the sale. Adding a small visual to let users know where they are in the checkout process is one way to improve the experience. Allowing users to save a shopping cart enables shoppers to take a break in the ordering process and return later without having to start over.

Security is another aspect of UX. To be successful, an online retail site must be secure. Users must be confident that their personal and credit card information will be used only in the ways that they intend. If a user suspects that a site is not secure, he or she will leave and go to a competitor. Having a HTTPS site, a more secure form of HTTP, is one way to show users that security is important. Retailers can also clearly post information about their security and privacy policies for customers to read.

Incorporating high-quality photos of products into a website can also improve user experience. Users live in a visual world. High-quality product photos give shoppers the feeling that they are picking out items in a store. Photos that show products being used or allow shoppers to zoom or rotate angles can make the online shopping experience feel as real as possible and encourages users to buy. Customer reviews about products are also helpful in improving the customer experience. However, sometimes less is more on a website. Too much text, photos, videos, or other content can clutter a webpage and distract a user from their ultimate goal—making a purchase.

WORKING AS A UX DESIGNER

As more companies realize the importance of creating the best user experience for customers, the area of UX design is growing. Laura Klein, author of *UX for Lean Startups*, described UX design in a September 2015 interview on UserTesting.com like this: "If UX is the experience that a user has while interacting with your product, then UX Design is, by definition, the process by which we determine what that experience will be. UX Design always happens. Whether it's intentional or not, somebody makes the decisions about how the human and the product will interact. Good UX Design happens when we make these decisions in a way that understands and fulfills the needs of both our users and our business." For online retail sites with many complex processes and interaction-based applications, good UX design can help keep customers coming back in the future.

UX designers work to improve a user's experience across all devices. They spend a lot of time thinking about how a person interacts with a website or other digital system. They look at factors such as ease of use, perception of value, efficiency, and more. They study the processes within a system or website. For example, they might study the checkout process of an online retail website to determine if users find the process intuitive and easy to use. They could also study the process of filling out a Web form to determine what the experience is like for users.

A UX designer tests a website from a customer's point of view and uses the information she gathers to make changes to improve the online experience.

Then they redesign and adjust the website or system to make it a better user experience.

Many times, the design process begins with user research. Using interviews and online surveys, UX designers gather data about user wants and needs. Using this data, UX designers create a wireframe or a rough sketch of each page and where the elements on each page should be placed. They can also create prototypes of web pages.

Once they have a prototype, UX designers test it with real users. They might observe users interacting with the site and ask them questions about the experience. A/B testing occurs when users receive two versions of the same page and the UX designer looks to see which version the user prefers. They can test the prototypes with users before the design is final and make any necessary changes. Once the site is live, the UX designer continually gathers feedback and makes adjustments to create a better user experience.

HOW TO BECOME A UX DESIGNER

UX design is a specialty within the broader area of web development. Most UX designers start with careers in web design or development. Most have at least an associate's degree in web design or a related field. For more technical jobs, some employers want employees to have at least a bachelor's degree in computer science, programming, or a related field. Some people interested in UX design choose to attend a boot camp or earn a certificate in UX design. These programs range from several days to several months. Some are in-person, while others can be completed online.

While writing code is not a requirement for all UX design jobs, having coding skills can make a candidate more attractive to employers. When UX designers know coding, they better understand the medium for which they are designing. They can more effectively communicate with web developers on the team. Coding skills in HTML, the markup language for making web pages, JavaScript, CSS, and other web languages are helpful for UX designers.

UX designers should have a solid understanding of graphic design and web technologies. They should be comfortable using design programs such as Photoshop, Illustrator, Fireworks, and InVision. They should also be able to use wireframing tools such as Axure RP and Balsamiq. Because the computer science environment is always changing, UX designers must continue to develop new computer skills and stay current on new tools and programming languages.

There is no substitute for real work experience to learn UX design. Working on a project with real users, team members, timeframes, and budgets is one of the best ways to learn UX design. To get this experience, some people volunteer for UX projects. They might help a local church or small business update its website. They offer to design or manage a website for a local conference. People already working in a tech position may be able to incorporate UX design into their current job. They might collect user feedback from a small group about a site's registration page. They can run a few usability tests and take notes.

UX designers gather for a team meeting to discuss changes that need to be made to a company website. In order to work well as a team, good communication is key.

Then they can share the result with their team.

Successful UX designers have excellent communication and interpersonal skills. Most work closely with others in a team. The work is often spread among team members, and the ability to work well with others and communicate is essential. In addition, UX designers must be able to communicate effectively with customers and use their feedback to improve the company's site and apps.

JOB OUTLOOK

The job outlook for the web development field and UX designers is very good. According to the Bureau of Labor Statistics' *Occupational Outlook Handbook,*

THE VALUE OF A MENTOR

A UX designer meets with her mentor over coffee to discuss her future goals and steps that she can take to help her achieve them.

A good mentor can help a person successfully navigate a UX design career. A mentor shares information about his or her own career path. He or she can give guidance, advice, and support for a person starting out in UX design. In a 2014 post on her website, UX designer Jessica Ivins said that having a mentor is an important step in becoming a successful UX designer. "Mentorship can be informal. Soak up everything an experienced UX designer can offer you. Ask someone a few questions at the next meetup. Take someone to lunch or coffee. Ask them to Skype with you for an hour," she said. However, Ivins cautions that a mentee should always be considerate of their mentor's time and not be overly demanding.

employment in the web development field is projected to grow 27 percent from 2014 to 2024. This rate of growth is much faster than the average of all occupations. In online retail, this growth is driven by the rapid increase in online platforms and services for consumers. As retail stores emphasize user experience, demand for UX design will also increase. In addition, the increasing use of mobile devices will also increase the number of opportunities as UX designers will be needed to create sites that work on mobile devices and multiple screen sizes. Candidates who have demonstrated UX experience, strong technical skills, and knowledge of multiple programming languages and digital multimedia tools will have the best opportunities for working as a UX designer in the online retail industry.

algorithm A set of rules followed in a calculation or other problem-solving activity, often performed by a computer.

beacon A wireless node that acts like a GPS locator and communicates with an app on a smartphone.

brick-and-mortar store A physical store location.

consumer A person who purchases goods and services.

data analytics The science of examining raw data and drawing conclusions from the information.

database A set of data held in a computer.

e-commerce Transactions that take place over the internet.

innovation A new method, process, or product.

interactive Allowing a two-way flow of information.

internship A temporary position that provides on-the-job training. It can be paid or unpaid.

marketing The act of promoting a business and selling products or services.

navigation The process of getting from one place to another.

node A central or connecting point.

prototype A first model of something, often used for testing.

responsive design The idea that web design should respond to a user's behavior and environment and should be able to be used on a variety of different devices and screen sizes.

retail The sale of goods to the public.

search engine optimization (SEO) A strategy to get a website listed higher on search engine lists.

statistics A branch of math that deals with analyzing and interpreting data and numbers.

streamline To make simpler and more efficient.

user experience (UX) How a person feels when he or she interacts with a system, website, mobile app, or software.

American Marketing Association
130 E. Randolph Street, 22nd Floor
Chicago, IL 60601
(800) AMA-1150
Website: https://www.ama.org
The American Marketing Association is a professional
association for marketing professionals. A section
of its website is devoted to digital marketing information and content.

Association of Software Professionals (ASP)
ASP Executive Director
PO Box 1522
Martinsville, IN 46151
(765) 349-4740
Website: http://asp-software.org
The ASP is a professional trade association of soft-
ware developers and provides a community for
software developers to share information about the
industry.

Information Technology Association of Canada
5090 Explorer Drive, Suite 510
Mississauga, ON L4W 4T9
Canada
(905) 602-8345
Website: http://itac.ca
The Information Technology Association of Canada
supports the development of a digital economy
in Canada. It represents information technology

professionals in a wide variety of industries, including online retail.

National Retail Federation (NRF)
1101 New York Avenue NW
Washington, DC 20005
(202) 783-7971
Website: https://nrf.com
The National Retail Federation (NRF) is the world's
largest retail trade association. It represents a variety of offline and online merchants from the United States and more than forty-five countries.

Retail Council of Canada
Toronto Office
1881 Yonge Street, Suite 800
Toronto, ON M4S 3C4
Canada
(416) 467-3777
Website: http://www.retailcouncil.org
The retail Council of Canada is a nonprofit, industry-funded association that represents more than forty-five thousand retail stores across Canada. Its website has links to a variety of resources, including industry news and research.

Retail Industry Leaders Association
1700 N. Moore Street, Suite 2250
Arlington, VA 22209
(703) 841-2300
Website: https://www.rila.org
The Retail Industry Leaders Association is a trade

association for leading retail companies. It provides educational and networking events for the retail industry.

WEBSITES

Because of the changing nature of internet links, Rosen Publishing has developed an online list of websites related to the subject of this book. This site is updated regularly. Please use this link to access the list:

http://www.rosenlinks.com/CYP/retail

FOR FURTHER READING

Abraham, Nikhil. *Coding for Dummies (For Dummies [Computer/Tech]).* Hoboken, NJ: John Wiley & Sons, 2016.

Belew, Shannon. *Starting an Online Business All-in-One for Dummies.* Hoboken, NJ: John Wiley & Sons, 2014.

Capala, Matthew. *SEO Like I'm 5: The Ultimate Beginner's Guide to Search Engine Optimization.* New York, NY: Zeit Media, 2014.

Kassnoff, David. *What Degree Do I Need to Pursue a Career in Information Technology & Information Systems?* New York, NY: Rosen Publishing, 2014.

La Bella, Laura. *Building Apps.* New York, NY: Rosen Publishing, 2015.

Lowe, Doug. *Java All-in-One for Dummies.* Hoboken, NJ: John Wiley & Sons, 2014.

Matthes, Eric. *Python Crash Course: A Hands-On, Project-Based Introduction to Programming.* San Francisco, CA: No Starch Press, 2015.

Niver, Heather. *Careers for Tech Girls in Computer Science.* New York, NY: Rosen Publishing, 2014.

Rosen Publishing. *Code Power: A Teen Programmer's Guide* (series). New York, NY: Rosen Publishing, 2015.

Spraul, V. Anton. *Think Like a Programmer: An Introduction to Creative Problem Solving.* San Francisco, CA: No Starch Press, 2012.

BIBLIOGRAPHY

Bensinger, Greg. "Shoppers Flock to Apps, Shaking Up Retail." *Wall Street Journal*, April 13, 2016. http://www.wsj.com/articles/shoppers-flock-to-apps-shaking-up-retail-1460539801.

Bowdon, Jason. "How the Top Brands Use Social Media for Marketing," Business 2 Business Community, September 7, 2014. http://www.business2community.com/social-media/top-brands-use-social-media-marketing-0995357#5yP-MrO9q8ugSZO4f.97.

eMarketer.com. "Shoppers Are Downloading More Mobile Retail Apps." June 3, 2016. http://www.emarketer.com/Article/Shoppers-Downloading-More-Mobile-Retail-Apps/1014041.

Gaudin, Sharon. "Neiman Marcus Wants to Merge the Online and In-Store Shopping Experience." *Computerworld*, January 19, 2016. http://www.computerworld.com/article/3024226/retail-it/neiman-marcus-wants-to-merge-the-online-and-in-store-shopping-experience.html.

Goldman, Sharon. "Why Data Scientist Is the Hottest Tech Job in Retail." *CIO*, April 13, 2016. http://www.cio.com/article/3055833/retail/why-data-scientist-is-the-hottest-tech-job-in-retail.html.

Infinity Technologies. "Toys Paradise." Retrieved 2016. http://www.infinitytechnologies.com.au/toys-para-dise. Infinity Technologies. "Toys Paradise." Retrieved 2016. http://www.infinitytechnologies.com.au/toys-paradise.

Ivins, Jessica. "My Advice for Becoming a UX

Designer." May 27, 2014. http://jessicaivins.net/
my-advice-for-becoming-a-ux-designer.

King, Mark. "A Working Life: The App Developer."
Guardian, March 5, 2011. http://www.
theguardian.com/money/2011/mar/05/
working-life-app-developer.

Lanoue, Spencer. "What Is UX Design? 15
User Experience Experts Weigh In." Using
Testing.com, September 16, 2015. https://
www.usertesting.com/blog/2015/09/16/
what-is-ux-design-15-user-experience-experts-weigh-in.

Lindner, Matt. "Online Sales Will Reach $523 Billion by
2020 in the U.S." Internet Retailer, January 29,2016.
http://www.internetretailer.com/2016/01/29/
online-sales-will-reach-523-billion-2020-us.

Morrison, Kimberlee. "12-Step Guide for
Social Media Marketing Success." *Adweek*,
October 5, 2016. http://www.adweek.com/
socialtimes/12-step-guide-for-social-media-market-
ing-success-infographic/645726.

Murray, Seb. "Growth in Online Channels Delivers
Retail Careers for MBAs." BusinessBecause,
December 1, 2014. http://www.business-
because.com/news/mba-careers/2948/
growth-in-online-delivers-retail-careers-for-mbas.

Perez, Sarah, "ClosetSpace Brings Fashion Inspiration
and Recommendations to Your Smartphone."
TechCrunch, January 14, 2015. https://techcrunch.
com/2015/01/14/closetspace-brings-fashion-inspi-
ration-and-recommendations-to-your-smartphone.

Reddy, Trips. "13 Retail Companies Using Data to
Revolutionize Online & Offline Shopping Experiences."

Umbel.com, May 18, 2015. http://www.umbel.com/
blog/retail/13-retail-companies-already-using-data-rev-
olutionize-shopping-experiences.

Schiff, Jennifer Lonoff. "12 Ways to Improve the
Customer Experience for Online Shoppers."
CIO, April 27, 2015. http://www.cio.com/
article/2914780/e-commerce/12-ways-to-im-
prove-the-customer-experience-for-online-shoppers.
html?page=2.

Stackpole, Beth. "Your Next Job: Mobile App Developer?"
Computerworld, June 27, 2011. http://www.comput-
erworld.com/article/2509463/app-development/
your-next-job--mobile-app-developer-.html?page=4.

Statista. "Percentage of U.S. Population with a Social
Media Profile from 2008 to 2016." 2016. https://
www.statista.com/statistics/273476/percent-
age-of-us-population-with-a-social-network-profile.

Suzuno, Melissa. "How to Find a Front-End Developer
Job: Chat with Mike Feineman, Lead Developer at
Room 214." After College.com, July 12, 2013. http://
blog.aftercollege.com/how-to-find-a-front-end-devel-
oper-job-chat-with-mike-feineman-lead-developer-at-
room-214.

Webley, Kayla. "A Brief History of Online Shopping." Time.
com, July 16, 2010. http://content.time.com/time/
business/article/0,8599,2004089,00.html.

Zeng, Brian. "5 Ways Online Retailers Can Make
Use of Big Data." Internet Retailer, February
6, 2015. https://www.internetretailer.com/
commentary/2015/02/06/5-ways-online-retailers-
can-make-use-big-data.

INDEX

ABOUT THE AUTHOR

Carla Mooney is a graduate of the University of Pennsylvania. Before becoming an author, she spent several years working in finance as an accountant. Today, she writes for young people and is the author of many books for young adults and children. Mooney enjoys learning about new technologies and the impact they will have on the retail industry and the average consumer. She is an avid online shopper and looks forward to Cyber Monday each year.

PHOTO CREDITS

Cover, p. 50 © iStockphoto.com/PeopleImages; p. 1 (background) Verticalarray/Shutterstock.com; p. 3 (background) Toria/Shutterstock.com; p. 5 Ritu Manoj Jethani/Shutterstock.com; p. 9 ESB Professional/ Shutterstock.com; p. 11 Dan Kitwood/Getty Images; p. 14 fotoinfot/ Shutterstock.com; p. 17 © iStockphoto.com/izusek; p. 19 Castleski/ Shutterstock.com; pp. 22, 31 baranq/Shutterstock.com; pp. 26, 66 Monkey Business Images/Shutterstock.com; p. 28 Eugenio Marongiu/ Shutterstock.com; p. 33 dotshock/Shutterstock.com; p. 37 ESB Essentials/Shutterstock.com; pp. 40–41 SFIO CRACHO/Shutterstock.com; p. 43 Peter Bernik/Shutterstock.com; p. 47 tulpahn/Shutterstock.com; p. 53 IB Photography/Shutterstock.com; p. 57 Agenturfotografin/ Shutterstock.com; pp. 60–61 © iStockphoto.com/vgajic; pp. 64–65 © iStockphoto.com/Geber86; back cover, pp. 4–5 (background) nadla/E+/Getty Images; interior background pages graphics pp. 8, 18, 36, 46, 56 (computer) Johan Swanepoel/Shutterstock.com, (binary code) Titima Ongkantong/ Shutterstock.com.

Designer: Michael Moy
Editor and Photo Researcher: Bethany Bryan

DATE DUE